CHIAROSCURO

a light and dark skin comedy

Aishah Rahman

BROADWAY PLAY PUBLISHING INC
New York
www.broadwayplaypublishing.com
info@broadwayplaypublishing.com

CHIAROSCURO

First printing: December 2010
Second printing: May 2013
I S B N: 978-0-88145-472-7

Book design: Marie Donovan
Page make-up: Adobe Indesign
Typeface: Palatino
Printed and bound in the U S A

ALSO BY AISHAH RAHMAN

Plays

LADY DAY A MUSICAL TRAGEDY
THE MOJO AND THE SAYSO
ONLY IN AMERICA
TALE OF MADAME ZORA
UNFINISHED WOMEN CRY IN NO MAN'S LAND
WHILE A BIRD DIES IN A GILDED CAGE

One Acts

Mingus Takes (3)
IF ONLY WE KNEW
THE LADY AND THE TRAMP
SPEAKER'S HEAD

Novel

Pigmentocracy Blues

Memoir

Chewed Water

Libretto

ANYBODY SEEN MARIE LAVEAU?

CHARACTER & SETTING

GINA ROSE, *"I want to get married....NOW!"*

RUSS, *looking for the right kind of woman*

NAYRON, *a former guest of the State and looking*

TILMAN, *sixty and just looking*

SIENNA, *fifty going on thirty*

LA HONDA DEJA VUE, *a black dumb blonde*

PAUL PAUL LEGBA, *Papa Legba, the African trickster spirit, disguised as a ship steward*

Aboard the deck of the cruise ship S S Chiaroscuro

PLAYWRIGHT'S NOTES

The visual in this play (as in life) speaks louder than any amount of words. All the women, except Gina Rose are very light with varying shades of blonde hair. The actress who plays Gina Rose should appear the lightest and the only one without blonde hair (preferably jet black long and straight hair and she could pass for Caucasian more than any of the other women). Sienna is the darkest of the women and yet she is barely brown. All the men, however, are *dark.* Paul Paul Legba, is very, very dark.

The word "pretty" is a euphemism for light skin and every time it is uttered it should hold an awesome weight in the speaker's mouth.

ACT ONE

Scene 1

(Aboard S S Chiaroscuro under a banner that reads, "Chocolate Singles.")

(All the characters pose as PAUL PAUL LEGBA*)*

LEGBA:*(Bowing deeply to audience)* Welcome to my ship. *(To the Chocolate Singles as he aims his camera)* All together now sayyy,

ALL: WE LOOK GOOD!

LEGBA: *(To* GINA*)* *Bon.* Now you. Solo.

GINA: Why me? I'm exhausted. I've had enough.

LEGBA: My camera insists.

tGINA: No! I hate taking pict—

LEGBA: Careful... My camera has an *eye* of her own. If you don't watch out she will reveal all your secrets. If I *were* you I would obey her.

GINA: *(Posing seductively)* Alright, alright.

ALL: *(Looking at* GINA*)* GIRL...YOU LOOK GOOD

LEGBA: All aboard on a romantic Singles Cruise to Nowhere. *Vous etes* truly *les belle noires.* Relive the glory days of ocean traveling, babies, grand slavers, elegant babies gourmet cusinie overboard. Relive the ambiance of *la belle epoque,* iron neck collars, beautiful jam-packed holes, graceful, branding irons refurbished, human stench, luxurious cruise ships ever built re-christened. Chiaroscuro offers a cruise experience guaranteed to take you back to the golden era of luxurious passenger travel. *Quel romantique!*

LA HONDA: Huh? What's he babbling about?

TILMAN: I don't understand a word you are saying.

RUSS: What language do you speak?

LEGBA: *Mo parle kreyole.* Sometimes.

GINA: Where are you from?

LEGBA: Yes.

LA HONDA: *(Whispering to the person next to her)* He *is* weird...and he *wasn't* listed in the travel brochure. Where is the Captain of this ship?

LEGBA: El Capitano is a bit shy. He speaka small English but sends welcome aboard greetings. El Capitano invites you to have dinner with him at El Capitano's Table. Eh?

LA HONDA: What *is* the Captain's name anyhow?

*(*LEGBA *bows deeply but does not answer.)*

LA HONDA: I want to report to the Captain that a piece of my luggage has been misplaced. The ones that contain my summer furs.

*(*LEGBA *gives another silent haughty low bow.)*

LA HONDA: A *lady* has to have her summer furs on a cruise, you know... Be sure to report this to your captain immediately. *(Whispering to the nearest person)* I can't stand this creature.

LEGBA: El Capitano has asked me to attend to your every romantic need, you Chocolate Singles, you! Tonight there will be a lucky stateroom draw and the winner will find

NAYRON: Several dead Presidents. This cruise ain't cheap.

LEGBA: —a gift of great value.

TILMAN: I know. A woman, ha, ha.

RUSS: A *pretty* woman.

NAYRON: On this ship there is no other kind. It's guaranteed

LEGBA: Yes, there will be one waiting under the winner's freshly pumped pillow.

LA HONDA: Underneath the pillow? A Kinky!

LEGBA: A CAMEO! Not quite. But it is priceless portrait of an ivory woman treasured around the world in every tribe, in every country, for her pale, delicate beauty carved against the blackest stone in nature.

(They pass the cameo to each other.)

VARIOUS:
I've never seen ivory so white.
The cameo woman's neck is so long, so thin.
Her hair is piled on top of her small head so high.

RUSS: To hold something so pale, so fair , in the palms of my hands...it's like flying...

TILMAN: How much does one of these cameos go for?

LEGBA: You couldn't afford it. You have to win it. Let the competition begin.

GINA: What about us? Don't the women get a prize?

LEGBA: Y'all are the prize..

RUSS: Steward...just what is your name?

LEGBA: *(Obsquiesouly bowing very low but managing to remain haughty)* Paul Paul Legba. Accent on the last syllable. What's yours?

LA HONDA: Oh! Your name is French, isn't it? Mind is too. La Honda. La Honda Deja Vue.

LEGBA: *Non!*

LA HONDA: Yes. I mean Oui..it is too.

LEGBA: I don't think so.

LA HONDA: It is too. You probably think it's Japanese, but it's Frencaise. Just like my middle name, which is Deja Vue.

LEGBA: *Vraiment?* Deja Vue? Hmmmmmmmm. Have I ever seen you before?

TILMAN: Forget him, La Honda. We are on the Love Boat. The moon is full and love is in our forecast.

LA HONDA: *(Looks at* RUSS *who is smiling at* GINA*)* You bet it is. Would you mind introducing me to

TILMAN: It seems to me that he is preoccupied. But my dear, have you ever considered a fine wine of mature age, not too dry, mature, full of youthful spice, smooth and mellow ...

SIENNA: *(To* LA HONDA*)* Careful, dearie. Old grapes make vinegary wine.

TILMAN: Sounds like sour grapes to me, my dear.

LA HONDA: Wine? Never touch the stuff. My drink is Tanqueray with a shot of

TILMAN: *(Ignoring* SIENNA*)* Aha! Just as I thought. A novice to the joys and wisdom of the grape. Let me teach you tonight. Steward...Legba...over here.... A liter of your finest wine so that I may toast the lady...

LEGBA: *Non.* Drink water. No drinks. Not right now. Later. Time to stoke the furnace, nouri l'esclaves, feed the Slaves. I leave you to regurgitmeditate the word is meditate. Yes...on the menu. *Mesdames, monsieurs.* I wish you a smooth, smooth trip.

*(*LEGBA*, bowing deeply, exits backwards as they all laugh.)*

RUSS: Eccentric.

GINA: Amusing.

LA HONDA: Annoying and rude. I say we have a meeting with the Captain of this ship right away! Besides, I need my summer furs!

(Music: You Stepped Out of a Dream*)*

RUSS: *(To* GINA*)* Hello.

GINA: I'm Gina Rose.

RUSS: Of course you are. Pretty could have no other name.

GINA: I just want you to know, I don't care what kind of problems you have. Drugs; alcohol, I'm willing to work with you.

RUSS: Let's dance.

*(*GINA *and* RUSS *dance perfectly together.)*

GINA: We know who we are.

RUSS: Where we are.

GINA: What time it is...

RUSS: Our numbers, our statistics.

GINA: Our loneliness.

RUSS: Shango man looking for Oshun woman to share his thunderbolts.

GINA: Like your cosmology. *(To audience)* What great neo-post modern Afro-centric 21st sex is this going to be! *(To* RUSS*)* S F M looking for S B M to share her quilt.

RUSS: *(To audience)* When you meet the right woman, you know it. There are no questions like, is there someone else out there, could I do better?"

(To GINA*)* I have status and money and intuition and it tells me right now you and I.

GINA: *(To audience)* Let. Him. Love. Me. Make this happen. I have done all this.

*(*LA HONDA *and NAYRON,* TILMAN *and* SIENNA *join in the dancing.)*

LA HONDA: *(To* RUSS *and* GINA*)* I see you two didn't waste no time.

NAYRON: Why should they? If it's a go, then kick it. Don't none of us need to wait for no Godot, hey bro?

TILMAN: She has just the right look somehow. I know it when I see it. *(To* SIENNA*)* Don't worry, darling. You got it too.

SIENNA: I'm not worried.

RUSS: *(To* GINA*)* Your teeth, your smile, your fair eyes.

LEGBA: *(To audience)* Fair eyes?

RUSS: *(To audience)* Ahhh I'm good at making money but not at poetry. You know what I'm trying to say, don't you?

LA HONDA: He's just trying to say, "WE LOOK GOOD."

RUSS: *(Gazing at* GINA*)* I could never resist a pretty woman.

*(*RUSS *sees* GINA *has turned green and is in obvious distress.)*

RUSS: Seasick already? We haven't even begun to sail.

(End of Scene 1)

Scene 2

(A few hours later. TILMAN *is in his stateroom unpacking.)*

TILMAN: *(To audience)* I'll give her to the count of five to knock and pretend she didn't know it was my roo

(A timid knock of the door)

TILMAN: *(To audience)* Sorry, I said five. I wanted to give her the benefit of the doubt.

(The knock, still timid, grows louder.)

TILMAN: Unpredictability was never one of her strong points. One.

(The knock. Still timid but more insistent now.)

TILMAN: Of course she would tell you monogamy was never mine. Two.

(The knock turns persistent now.)

TILMAN: I must say she's looking good. For a woman of our age. Three.

(The knock is pitiful and full of tears.)

TILMAN: I'm giving her time to breathe. Four.

*(*TILMAN *breathes deeply as there comes a desperate knock)*

TILMAN: Five. *(He finally opens the door.)*

SIENNA: Oh...I didn't know...I was looking for someone else—I—I didn't know this was—

TILMAN: We're not strangers, so come in.

SIENNA: It is you. At first I couldn't, wouldn't—belie—

TILMAN: It's been such a long time—

SIENNA How long has it been since you and I—

TILMAN: So many years. I thought we were both dead!

(A moment of laughter.)

SIENNA: Tilman Gandy, quick with the lip but not slow to go.

TILMAN: *(Still laughing, says to audience)* Here we go...

SIENNA: I've kept up with you and your marriages... heard bits and pieces through friends...and...others.

TILMAN: *(Trying to keep it light)* How ironic. You and I accidentally running into each other on a singles cruise.

SIENNA: "Rosebushy?" You just...called—

TILMAN: No...I, I didn't...did I? I did.... My tongue got trapped...in a time warp—I didn—

SIENNA: "Strong Oak" and "Rosebushy" couldn't get enough of each other...once....

TILMAN: Have a drink, Sienna. I really meant Sienna. You still go by that name, don't you? I don't know what anybody's name is these days.

SIENNA: You are so right... "Rasaba."

TILMAN: Oh ha ha ha right. "Rasaba."

SIENNA: Your warrior name. Those were the days.

TILMAN: You realize those days were in the last century?

SIENNA: B C: before computers, when jazz was still ethnic music and you and I were together.

TILMAN: You look good. I even think you look... I don't know...

*(*SIENNA *is quiet as he struggles.)*

TILMAN: What have you done to yourself?

*(*SIENNA *is still quiet.)*

TILMAN: I don't know what it is. There's something about you that's well...different. It's something I can't quite— You are— Maybe but.... No. No. It's not that either, you— More like the women in the theaters and magazines...someone a man can show off to the world and say, "Look what I'm humping" and less like.... what was it you used to call me... "Burnt Sienna?"

TILMAN: Ohhhhhhh. You always so sensitive.

SIENNA: I have to go. Sorry to knock on your door uninvited. It was mistake.

TILMAN: Maybe I can help—who were you—lookin

SIENNA: I told you I was looking for—

TILMAN: Yes... who.. you were looking for.

SIENNA: *(Going toward the door)* That's okay... I'll find it. Don't worry... See you...

TILMAN: So how are you? Really. I mean it. How are you?

SIENNA: Surprised to see you. What are you doing he—

TILMAN: Cruising... What else on a Singles Cruise. And you?

SIENNA: . *(Pause)* You're the last person I would expect to see. Here, I mean.

TILMAN: Why not? I'm single

SIENNA: —Yes, so I heard. Don't worry— You won't stay that way for long. You're a man.

TILMAN: I'm not worried.... That's why I'm here. Why should I stay by myself if I don't have to?

SIENNA: *(To audience)* Yes. Why should he? James Brown was so right. It is a man's world. *(To* TILMAN*)* Yes. Why should you? But I would think this type of... crowd would be...a bit provincial...for you.

TILMAN: Soooo. What are you doing for yourself? Still teaching?

SIENNA: I really must go....

TILMAN: Where...what cabin number did you say you were looking for?

SIENNA: I really should go.

TILMAN: What happened?

SIENNA: Happened?

TILMAN: To teaching...I heard you had some trouble at your college

SIENNA: What? ...Nothing. Nothing. *(Pause)* I seduced one of my students. Afterwards I gave him an "A" and told him he never had to come to class. The other students were jealous. They wanted "A"s also, but they couldn't measure up.

*(*SIENNA *and* TILMAN *both crack up.)*

SIENNA: I may be funny, but I'm not kidding. After you left I was so lonely.

TILMAN: So it was my fault? *(To audience)* With her, everything is my fault.

SIENNA: You asked. I told you. I know my reality is hard for you to comprehend. *(To audience)* I'm talking but he doesn't hear. As usual.

TILMAN: This person.

SIENNA: What person?

TILMAN: The one you were looking for when you knocked on my door. By mistake...of course.

SIENNA: I hope you didn't think that I intended to kn—

TILMAN: No... I don't think tha—

SIENNA: Ohhhh. Yes. You know who I was looking for?

TILMAN: Enlighten *moi.*

SIENNA: The...the CAPTAIN. I want to see the captain of this ship.

TILMAN: The Captain? C'mon Sienna...You can do better than that. The only time we can expect to see the Captain is if we are lucky enough to be invited to dine at his table—you can't just go knocking on the Captain's cabin door.

SIENNA: Why not? I paid top dollar to take this cruise.

TILMAN: You want a refund already? *(He cracks up.)*

SIENNA: It's not that funny. Besides there's something wron—this boat is headed in the wrong direction..we are going east instead of west.

TILMAN: What difference does it make? Remember this is a cruise to Nowhere. East... West... North... South... It doesn't make any difference. Remember... We're going Nowhere.

SIENNA: How many days it takes to get there?

TILMAN: Oh just relax. I just booked the trip and got on.

SIENNA: Yeah? But what I want to know is.... How long does it take to get to nowhere?

TILMAN: *(Seized by a pain in the gut which he tries to hide. To audience)* Every night I ask myself that same question. *(To* SIENNA*)* I don't care and neither do you. Cmon, admit it. A man and woman on the sea is the stuff romance is made of. That's why were here. It doesn't matter what direction we take.

SIENNA: I just like to find out the small details like where we're going—how long—stuff like that. You know me.

TILMAN: Yeah. I know you. I knew you and I want you to know that I think about you. *(He rummages around underneath his pillow searching for something.)*

SIENNA: Me too.

TILMAN: Wait a minute... just let me see something....

(Lifts his pillow and sees the cameo) I'll be damned. I won her I won her I WON!

SIENNA: Aoh...her...

TILMAN: Yeah. The jewel, the prize the gem the fair Cameo... Damn Sienna you brought me luck .

SIENNA: Glad to be of use

TILMAN: Legend has it that only pretty women can wear a cameo. My mother never got dressed up without her cameo brooch. I used to think it was her portrait carved in ivory.

SIENNA: Your mother I heard she...

TILMAN: Two years ago...this June..

SIENNA: I'm sorry. I always liked her, even though she didn't li...

TILMAN: Mother liked everybody.

SIENNA: C'mon...I knew she always thought I was too d

TILMAN: *(Laughing)* That didn't mean she disliked you. She just had some traditional ways.

SIENNA: Question is whose tradition? What tradition?

TILMAN: C'mon Sienna, you know how the old folks are.

SIENNA: Young ones too...and those in between. Very, very traditional.

TILMAN: *(Grimacing with a flash of pain and tries to hide it.)* Maybe Cameo will change my luck. It's nothing... Just indigestion. I guess it's time to stop eating swine... *(Pause)* ...I've got something, to ask you.

SIENNA: I was wondering if you ever thought about it.

TILMAN: I think about it every day. Is she or isn't she?

SIENNA: She's eighteen...you're asking...now?

TILMAN: Is she or isn't she?

SIENNA: Here's her graduation picture. What do you think?

TILMAN: I can't tell. Could be mine. Could be his. That's what you told me...those were your own words when you found out you were pregnant.

SIENNA: *(Laughing)* Both of you tripped over each other in your panic to get away from me.

TILMAN: I had married her by then... He was married also.

SIENNA: Right...you had left me for Heather...and he was with Brittany.

(Pause)

TILMAN: All troubled water under a bridge.

SIENNA: Or is it troubled bridge over troubled waters?

*(*TILMAN *is laughing but not happy.)*

SIENNA: I lived in a fantasy world . Taking the left over crumbs you both offered me and pretend it was love-making.

TILMAN: His or mine?

SIENNA: I pretended when I was with either one of you that I was not just practice material for your main event.

TILMAN: His or mine?

SIENNA: What difference does it make...now?

TILMAN: His or mine?

SIENNA: You once told me, "It's not my baby, Sienna. She's all yours."

TILMAN: His or mine?

SIENNA: His.

TILMAN: I don't know whether to be relieved or sad. *(Pause)* You never married?

SIENNA: Ask me!

TILMAN: Whaaaa?

SIENNA: I want you to ask me to marry you. Or pretend to. Just to hear how it sounds. Cmon now...say it...

TILMAN: No. This is silly.

SIENNA: No it is not. I have been pregnant five times, had two abortions, given a child up for adoption and raised a daughter by myself. And I have yet to hear a man's voice asking me to marry him. I just wanna hear how it sounds.

TILMAN: I'm sorry those things happened to you but don't bla

SIENNA: Ask me. Just make believe. C'mon, it can't hurt. "Will you marry me, Sienna?" Go ahead...I just pretend...I used to pretend with you. Remember?

TILMAN: But I had nothing to do with the...

SIENNA: *I* did a lot of pretending with *you*. I'm just asking you this one thing, for old times sake.

TILMAN: No—you and I might have a history but one thing I don't believe in is guilt.

SIENNA: *(Trying on different voices)* Will you marry me/ will you marry me, Sienna will you marry me? Darling will you marry marry me , honey pie will you marry marry marry marry marry, me sweet...

TILMAN: Sienna. This isn't funn—

SIENNA: C'mon. Will you marry me, will you marry me, will you marry me? *(Going to the door)* I just wanted to hear what all those other women heard when you asked them. Can't even pretend with me?

TILMAN: I don't see the poin— I mean, what's the point, woman?

SIENNA: The point...Tilman Gandy is that I have raised your daughter—without any assistance from you...

TILMAN: My daughter!!!!! But you just said—

SIENNA: Of course she's yours. As if you didn't know. I've been telling you for years. Once she was born I knew you were her father. And I told you and told you and when you left town I wrote to you and wrote to you...and you denied and denied...til I finally one day...I stopped.

TILMAN: I wasn't sure....

SIENNA: There are ways to be sure...if you want....

TILMAN: But just a minute ago you just said...

SIENNA: Why should I give you the gift of her after all the hard work is done?

TILMAN: She's grown...in college....

SIENNA: Do you even know her name?

TILMAN: If you were so sure I'm the father and this is true, why didn't you take me to court?

SIENNA: I didn't think that would have added dignity to her life—or mine. Or yours.

TILMAN: I...I...I...

SIENNA: "Phoenix Aurora...the dawn that rises from the ashes."

TILMAN: What?

SIENNA: You and I were so into names once in our lives, remember, Strong Oak? Your daughter's name. Just in case you wanted to know...is Phoenix Aurora... The dawn that rises from the ashes. I mean Tilman, Rasaba, Strong Oak, do you think you can get it up to just pretend to ask me to marry you?

(End of Scene 2)

Scene 3

(Sun deck. GINA *and* RUSS *sitting together.* LA HONDA, *a few deck chairs aways, stares at them.* TILMAN *enters.)*

TILMAN: *(To audience)* Have you ever seen a mermaid? I did. And I been crossing the waters ever sinceLooking for a mermaid. She look just like the picture books, Lovely fish tail, eyes blue as the Carribean sea and pale wet skin. *(Doubles over in the clutch of sudden pain, then slowly straightens up)* I'm an old street fighter and The Butcher got a fight on His hands until... Until... the...the final cut down ahAhhh *(Doubled over in pain again)* Ahhhh...shit! *(When the pain releases him, he begins to box his invisible foe.)* C'mon you bastard...fight like a man. Put your dukes up. This cruise is good for what ails me. Sea water and pretty women. That was my mother's remedy. It all starts with mothers. Mine believed in sea water and urine... "Boy, you complaining you throat's on fire? Here—take this cup of sea water and pee in it, gargle with it and shut up about it boy. No time to be sick." "Boy, teacher say you got a rash and you gotta go to the doctor? No such a thing. A good soak in your own pee. mixed with sea water cure. you of alto datl" It worked It really did, but I just learned to keep my illnesses to myself. *(Pause)* If only sea water and urine could cure what I got now ails me now. My mother would love to see me on this ship surrounded by the sea and pretty women. "If only she were with me now. *(Pause. In his mother's voice)* "Son, you got to keep up the family tradition." My mother was a great beauty. So was her mother before her. *(In his mother's voice)* "Fair loveliness runs in our family, so keep up the tradition." *(Pause)* From boyhood...I always associate the sea with pretty women. *(He joins* LA HONDA.*)* What luck. I was hoping to see a mermaid this morning.

(LA HONDA *does not even bother to look at him.)*

TILMAN: Will you join me for breakfast?

(LA HONDA *keeps on staring at* RUSS *and* GINA.)

TILMAN: I'm a well traveled man. Been all over. Eaten a cheese dog steak in Nebraska, flapjacks in Los Angeles, bufalo toes in Texas, cow balls in Montana.

(LA HONDA *still silent, staring at* RUSS *and* GINA.)

TILMAN: I eat the food of wherever I find myself. *(Pause)* I just have one rule about eating...and sex. *(Pause)* Never do it alone.

(Still no reaction from LA HONDA.)

TILMAN: La Honda. Yesterday you were brash and sassy. This morning you're like a seashell, silent on the outside, thunderous on the inside, delicate, brittle, pink and tan and sunbleached...will you marry me?

LA HONDA: *(Still looking at* RUSS) You are a real first class nut

TILMAN: A grand church wedding or City Hall. Your choice...but you better hurry up and decide. Let's not waste any time.

LA HONDA: Go pick on someone your own age.

TILMAN: I like *you.*

LA HONDA: And I like *him.*

TILMAN: And he likes *her*. *(Pause)* The first rule of a shipboard romance is to cast where the fish are biting.

LA HONDA: Then why don't you follow it?

TILMAN: *(To audience)* That's exactly what I'm doing. The fish is biting while she thinks she is fighting. I'm about to reel her in.

LA HONDA: What's she got that I haven't?

TILMAN: Him.

LA HONDA: I'm serious. Beauty is my business. Can't he see, I'm beautiful too. We've both got what he wants.

TILMAN: And...what is that...?

LA HONDA: Oh...you know...

TILMAN: No...you tell me..

LA HONDA: You know

TILMAN: Give me the 4-1-1, please.

LA HONDA: You know, Mister Gandy.... *(Touching her bare skin)*

TILMAN: There are other things....

LA HONDA: Get serious, Mister Tilman Are you trying to tell me at this moment in our acquaintance you have the hots for my sweet disposition?

TILMAN: Let's discuss it over lunch.

LA HONDA: Mister Gandy...

TILMAN: Tilman...

LA HONDA: You and I are born in different centuries . What could we talk about?

TILMAN: We could learn from one another. I could teach you...

LA HONDA: I'm looking for a romance...not a history teacher.

(Enter LEGBA *who bows before* TILMAN.*)*

LEGBA: Good morning sir

TILMAN: Could I...er...get a drink?

LEGBA: Certainly, sir. What shall I get you, sir?

TILMAN: A scotch.

LEGBA: Any soda-water, sir?

TILMAN: No. Thank you.

LEGBA: Scotch, straight, sir?

TILMAN: Every morning, As a matter of fact, steward, I'm warning you...you'll probably see a lot of me during this trip.

LEGBA: Your warning is an honor, sir.

TILMAN: Look here, how long before we sail?

LEGBA: Sail? We have been sailing...all night, sir.

TILMAN: Oh?? Never mind me. I had a damn thick night last night.

LEGBA: Yes, sir.

TILMAN: As a matter of fact...I've forgotten the ship's itinerary...just where is it we're cruising to...this gorgeous morning...

LEGBA: Yes, sir...it is a gorgeous morning. Your scotch is coming right up, sir.

*(*LEGBA *exits, but not before glancing at* LA HONDA *indifferently.)*

LA HONDA: *(To audience)* Did you see that? It was like I am invisible. Like I belong in third class or something. He didn't even bother to ask what the lady wanted.

*(*TILMAN, *silent, stares at the sea.)*

LA HONDA: *(Returning her attention to* RUSS *and* GINA*)* I would kill for him to look at me that way.

TILMAN: Thanks.

LA HONDA: I'd kill to have someone look at me that way.

TILMAN: You can't see the forest for the trees.

LA HONDA: What?

TILMAN: I said being in love can be hard on your knees.

LA HONDA: Knees?

TILMAN: I may appear to be standing, but my heart is kneeling to your fair loveliness.

LA HONDA: Is it true you were famous...some kind of musician back in the day. I heard you were big in Europe or something.

TILMAN: I been famous three or four times. On two or three continents.

LA HONDA: How come I never heard of

TILMAN: Probably did. Just didn't know it was me.

LA HONDA: What kind of music?

TILMAN: Jazz.

LA HONDA: Oh...did you make any mo

TILMAN: Not near as much as I should have. But enough to take you—

LA HONDA: Listen, Tilman. I was curious, that's all, and I'm not really interested in your more— I was hoping to find a husband...

TILMAN: I asked you to marry me, remember? I was not joking.

LA HONDA: I was hoping to find a man with, with class who could see the real me. I'm not just young, glamorous and beautiful . I'm also a caring...and... and sincere and love to hike and swim and fireside evenings. A young successful man with lots of, of class. That's all

TILMAN: So your answer is no. You wouldn't consider having lunch with an old musician who's made enough to take you on a shopping spree.

LA HONDA: Tilman, you're a sweet old gent—but I'm young and I want a chance at the

TILMAN: I've got something for you. Close your eyes.

(As LA HONDA *closes her eyes* TILMAN *puts the cameo in her hands.)*

LA HONDA: Tilman, you won it.

TILMAN: It's yours.

LA HONDA: I can, you don't nee...I don't want...I mean this is not junk jewelry. It's expen

TILMAN: This portrait of a pretty woman favors you girl. It's yours.

LA HONDA: *(Silent for a few beats.)* You know how to get to me. Don't you? I'll go get ready for lunch.

TILMAN: Don't rush away. Stay and talk with me.

LA HONDA: Can't. The sun is getting too strong.

TILMAN: It's early yet. The sun is barely risen.

LA HONDA: It's strong enough to burn.

TILMAN: Fear of cancer?

LA HONDA: Fear of suntan...I get very...you know quickly... But you can stay... You are a man. With men dark is sexy.

TILMAN: *(Looking at his dark arm with amusement)* Don't forget to think about what I asked you.

LA HONDA: What was that?

TILMAN: Will you marry me?

(End of Scene 3)

Scene 4

(The gentle lapping of the sea against the meandering ship. RUSS *and* GINA *enter holding hands. They are wearing bathing suits and beach robes of the same fabric and color. He puts his arm around her as she lays her head on his shoulder. Both face the audience, looking out at the sea.)*

GINA: So, how many gorgeous, incredible-looking women in your life?

RUSS: Shhhhhhh.

GINA: I don't mean in your whole life. Not even you immediate past. I mean now. How many at this very minute that you and I are standing looking out at the sea?

RUSS: The sea belongs to us now, Gina.

GINA: I was only kidding. I really don't want to know.

RUSS: This morning there is no one in the world but you and I and this big blue mirror milled the sea. A big, blue, smooth as glass mirror. Look. Right there, over there. See me going fishing? Got my best fly rod and a bottle of grasshoppers. Not the ordinary, black, sooty hoppers, but the beautiful pale iridescent ones with yellow wings. It is early morning, the river is clean and sparkling. I'm wading in it. I'm following the sun upstream where it is dangerous to fish. I like to go away, far away from the safe, shallow water where the dark trout swim. Upstream, I cast my rod against the current, against the mainstream, and haul in a bright, sparkling, pale fish. She is beautiful. Upstream in dangerous waters, against the current, where fishing could be tragic, I have caught a trophy. I am tired, but nothing, no one can touch me now. It is done and I have won.

GINA: I love the water.

RUSS: I love your hair.

GINA: All my life I have been a stranger in my own body.

RUSS: I love the way it looks, the way it feels, the way it smells. The way it tastes when I kiss each strand.

GINA: But...since...I...met...I mean...I don't feel strange to myself...anymore.

RUSS: I love to wet every inch of your scalp with my tongue.

GINA: This is the happiest night of my

RUSS: There is no— Only you, Gina. Only one true woman. You truly pretty woman.

END OF ACT ONE

ACT TWO

Scene 1

(NAYRON *and* SIENNA *sit alone on the deck.)*

NAYRON: Hey, mama!

SIENNA: I am not your mother.

NAYRON: I know, mama

SIENNA: I said

NAYRON: You look unhappy. Why should a good-looking female like you be sad.

SIENNA: I'm not sad. I'm made. I guess I am sad/mad.

NAYRON: Aw, mama. Anything I can do?

SIENNA: Young man, will you pl

NAYRON: Sorry. Just tryin to tell you—

SIENNA: Young man, leave me

NAYRON: —that I been peeping you.

SIENNA: —ALONE.

NAYRON: —with your fine, pretty self.

SIENNA: Young man, thanks for your solicitude. But you don't have to waste precious time talking to me. This is a singles cruise.

NAYRON: I know that, Miss Einstein. Miss, ain't it?

SIENNA: Yes, but....

NAYRON: I get it. You not into ex-cons? You not even interested enough to rap with me, hun? To conversate?

SIENNA: Young man, I—

NAYRON: I'm a great conversator.

(Silence from SIENNA*)*

NAYRON: What do you think about the Congress, police brutality, the class struggle, or the 21st Century?

SIENNA: Young man, I

NAYRON: Nayron. My name. Sounds like "Ray-on" or "Day-cron."

SIENNA: Nayron. What does it mean?

NAYRON: Stronger than silk. Softer than cotton. Born in nature, but new and improved. Nayron.

SIENNA: Young man. Nayron. Like I was saying, Nayron. You are a young man.

NAYRON: Is that a problem with you?

SIENNA: Look, youn—Nayron. Why do you want to talk with me?

NAYRON: Me man. You woman.

SIENNA: But I am older than—

NAYRON: Who's count—

SIENNA: —A lot older.

NAYRON: Don't worry. They tell me in women, it's the face that goes first.

SIENNA: What are you talking about?

NAYRON: I'm talking about you, mommi. They say in women, it's the face that goes first. Your face ain't gone no place...so the rest of you must be smoking!

(SIENNA *is silent, but pleased in spite of herself.)*

NAYRON: How old are you anyway?

SIENNA: *(Pauses for a couple of beats.)* I'd rather tell you my weight.

NAYRON: Which is—??

SIENNA: Listen, young man.

NAYRON: Nayron.

SIENNA: What do you want with me? Do you have some kind of incurable disease? Are you looking for a nurse? Or a purse?

NAYRON: You're much too pretty to be so cynical.

SIENNA: Comes with the territory. I may look young, but I'm not new. Been around the block a couple of times.

NAYRON: But you still have a heart with passion and innocence.

SIENNA: Yes.

NAYRON: I know. That's the first thing I peeped in you. Passion and innocence.

SIENNA: How did you act so...insightful.

NAYRON: Doing time at the Big Sky—

SIENNA: The Big Sky? Oh, you mean...

NAYRON: Yeah...the joint. That's all you see.

SIENNA: What were you in for?

NAYRON: I shot at someone. If I wanted to I could have killed him. I just wanted to scare someone who was fuckin with me.

SIENNA: How does it feel to be out?

NAYRON: I am very anxiety-ridden, shall I say. When I get on the subway, I look all up and down the motherfucker and I'm the only black person, male or female, in the car and I'm thinking, "these suckers could kill me and say I tried to hurt somebody." But then I'm glad I have my job cause my family ain't got no money and I gotta have a job, but it pisses me off when my supervisor says to me, "I can't believe you are as nice as you pretend to be, or are you just waiting, marking time." I get enraged, but of course I can't say anything. *(Pause)* Can you and I hang out?

SIENNA: Y'know. I routinely have background checks done on guys I date. To see if they have criminal records.

NAYRON: Aren't you glad I saved you the trouble... oh, I forgot to tell you about my B W B citations.

SIENNA: B W B. You mean D W B?

NAYRON: No...I mean B W B. I been cited a hundred and fifty times.

SIENNA: *One hundred fifty times?!* For what?

NAYRON: I told you. B W B.... Breathing while black.

SIENNA: *(Laughing)* That doesn't count.

NAYRON: So glad, Your Honor , so glad.

SIENNA: But I gotta tell you. I firmly believe in capital punishment.

NAYRON: No problem. Like I said, I don't do murder. Just a little mayhem.

*(*NAYRON *and* SIENNA *laugh and he suddenly tries to place something in her hand.)*

NAYRON: I want you to have it. It's a piece of good luck I found...underneath my pillow last night.

SIENNA: The Cameo! But...you couldn't...I...mean some—

NAYRON: Please let me give—

SIENNA: But...but it isn't...it couldn't.

NAYRON: Please. I want to...

SIENNA: But...

NAYRON: When someone gives a gift, it makes a bond between you.

SIENNA: What's our bond?

NAYRON: Coming together at this moment on this night, in this moment of our deep need...for... company...for understanding...for tenderness. The pull between us is as strong as the tide that rocks this ship. *(Pause)* No matter what happens between two people, a gift represents a moment of love. *(Pause)* I been thinking a lot about women. Before I did time, I never really thought about what women added to the world. A world without women would be crazy. Sure, some of you females are as messed up in the head as any man, but all things considered, women, in most cases, know more about human beings than most men I come across. *(Pause)* Women bring a lot to the table that the world can't do without. Every man has his ideal woman. Without that picture, doing time would be impossible. But when you in the joint you settle... you settle for the woman who makes the long trip, for the woman who has your baby. For the woman who needs you to act like you are a man, you are sincerely grateful. *(Pause)* But when I was in the joint, I kept a picture of Marilyn on the wall. I kept her before me at all times. Before my baby's momma would visit I used to fantasize that it was really Marilyn and after she would leave I wouldgaze at her picture hoping she would step down from the wall and settle in my cell. She was like my altar. *(Pause)* But now I'm a free man, mama and I'm here, talking to you.

(End of Scene 1)

Scene 2

(Interior of GINA*'s cabin. She is in her thong bathing suit. She carefully tapes a huge picture of the sun to the wall. She wraps herself in strips of cloth, twisting round and round, twisting her body as she speaks.)*

GINA: *(To herself)* I see...that there...is only one way... one way...only to sunbathe properly... It's not the tan... that...counts... It's the tan lines.... "Before" suntan lines...and lots...and lots...and lots...and lots...and lots...and lots...of "Before" lines with a little sun tan in between. Otherwise...you take an awful chance... know what I mean? *(Finished and resembling a mummy bound in strips holding a suntan oil bottle up, she faces audience. To audience)* LINES!

(End of Scene 2)

Scene 3

*(*RUSS *is sitting on a deck chair. He jumps up suddenly to rush off when* LA HONDA *appears out of nowhere, blocking his way.)*

RUSS: Excuse—

LA HONDA: My fault. I'm La Honda, remember? Chow.

RUSS: Excuse me...kinda in a hurry...

LA HONDA: Here's my business card. Can I have yours?

RUSS: *(He reaches in his shorts and pulls out a business card.)* Listen, I'd love to stay, but I'm on my way to the men's...

LA HONDA: I just wanted to connect with you and say "chow".

RUSS: "Chow???"

LA HONDA: Y'know, Italian for hello.

RUSS: *(Laughing in spite of himself)* Ohhhh. You mean "*ciao*". That means goodbye.

LA HONDA: Whatever. It wouldn't be the first time I heard the words "hello" and "goodbye" in the same breath.

RUSS: I gotta go.

LA HONDA: See what I mean.

RUSS: Noo, noo, don't get me wrong, it's just that I really do have to go.

LA HONDA: I was wondering if you could advise me on some...stock. I hear you are very...successful. You look like you are...successful.

RUSS: Any other time I would love to talk business with you, but—

LA HONDA: I'm only asking for your advice because I'm a business woman myself.

RUSS: I gotta admit, businesswomen are sexy, but right now I—gotta go.

LA HONDA: I really want to talk to you.

RUSS: Gotta jet, sweetheart. It's an...emergency.

LA HONDA: I'm a salon owner. Turn over real good profits.

RUSS: Oh? What's the name of your...salon?

LA HONDA: Uh...La beaute...what else, I speak French as you know, La Beaute Inc. More than one. A chain. I mean, it's gonna be. A franchise, even. But right now I freelance. I'm a freelance manicurist. I got my own website though.

RUSS: Like I said...gotta split. I would really appreciate it if you let me pass. I really must go—

LA HONDA: *(Grabbing both his hands)* Lemme see your hands. I want to read you nails... Hmmmmmtnm... Just what I thought. You nail bed is big...wide...strong and thick. Good shape. Good color. Healthy. You been eating lots of the right things. I like a man who does that. Y'know? There's nothing I like better than feeling a man burst inside of me. I don't go for all kinky sex... well, maybe just a little, but all those whips and chains and dildos are just a little bit too continental for me. Good plain old dick and pussy is just fine. I don't even like to be spanked. Well, maybe just a li'l bit.... sometimes.

RUSS: La Honda! I don't even know you.

LA HONDA: I don't know you. Isn't that why we're all here. To get to know each other?

RUSS: Yes, but...

LA HONDA: Too fast forward and bold, huh? Well, you know the deal with We the People. That's what happens when the girls outnumber the boys. The uneven numbers among us has speeded up the natural flow of human emotions among us. No time to play games and be shy.

RUSS: La Honda... What do you want...from me?

LA HONDA: Are you gonna make believe you didn't see me staring at you all the time you were with her?

*(*RUSS *begins to smile in a strained manner,)*

LA HONDA: I can tell by the way you're smiling that she gave her measly breasts to you. You sucked them till she opened her legs and you walked right in without a thought of me.

RUSS: Actually, I'm not smiling. I'm just concentrating on keeping my bladder from exploding.

LA HONDA: Aw, c'mon Russ.

RUSS: *(Making a mad dash past her to the men's room)* Let me by, woman. My bladder....

LA HONDA: *(Leaning against the closed men's room door, half crying and talking to herself)* I want you to know one thing... *(Pause)* Even though I lead with my pu—body...I know, I know, that... *(Pause)* ...I know that.... *(Pause)* Sex...between two people...can be...such a...such a damned...*lonely* thing.

(End of Scene 3)

Scene 4

(An auctioneer's table. On the table are grotesque female dolls euphemistically known as "black collectibles". LEGBA *struts out dressed like a Southern auctioneer and raps to the audience. As he describes each doll, furious bidding between* LA HONDA, NAYRON, RUSS, SIENNA, *and* TILMAN.*)*

LEGBA: Yo chocolate hue jokers this auction is just for you. Yo you cruisers have ou met your mate no losers on this special date from the special collection of losers with those of impeccable nostalgia without neuralgia, history with histrionics. Yo hair is nappy and here is you mammy, one old painted metal mammy doorstop, you weave needs tighten, you need to lighten, one grinning fat, black mammy with milk flowing from her tits into a pail that says "Free Lunch" one coal kinky hair rubba doll with melon mammy "beauty coon." Yo ho bitch and da ho and do bitch which is witch, tabit and wsitch I'm gonna bring ya one "so you thing you been through the wringer" hard-working mammy with her tits caught in the washing machine ashtray, bid 'em in bid 'em out ovah here ovah there, straight up jetting into the strat-o-sphere. Baybee!

(As RUSS, TILMAN, *etc. violently bid over the "dolls," they become physical and in the melee the dolls are decapitated,*

dismembered, mutilated, but with their grotesque facial expressions intact.)

LEGBA: Sold to American!

GINA: *(To audience)* Are you sure this is only a dream?

END OF ACT TWO

ACT THREE

*(*GINA *enters. She is wearing revealing beach wear that highlights her suntan lines.)*

*(*GINA *walks over to* RUSS, *who is alone, sitting, contemplating the ocean. She enters carrying a garland of flowers. She places herself behind him and places the garland on top of this head.)*

GINA: I crown you King of Love. Think how you love me tonight. Remember tonight. Remember, somewhere inside me there will always be the person that I am tonight.

(As the garland falls below RUSS*'s waist and lays in his lap he closes his eyes and reaches behind him to clasp his hands around* GINA*'s neck She enfolds her arms around his chest.)*

RUSS: I'll always... We'll always...

GINA: *(Interrupting)* Shh. For now...if not always.

RUSS: For always and now...

(The band begins to play Samba Saravah *and* LEGBA *appears, dancing in the background, circling the couple as their lovemaking silently progresses.)*

LEGBA: *Sa se ya pele mizik mem*. That's what they call playing real music! *(He begins to sing the words from* Samba Saravah *as he dances around them.)* Happiness is more or less what we seek I like to laugh and sing and I don't speak
Against nice people having a good time

Dancing a samba without sadness.
Is like loving a woman who is no more than beautifu.
I know some people who find songs a bore,
For others they're a fashion and nothing more,
And for still others money's the only thing.

Searching out their roots on foreign ground,
If the deepest roots are to be found
Then it's the samba-song that we must sing.

It first came from Bahia, rumor goes.
Its rhythm and its poetry it owes
To centuries of dancing and of pain.

But whatever the feelings it combines,
Although it maybe white in form and rhymes,
Its heart is black as black and that is plain.
Its heart is black as black and that is plain.

(End of Scene 1)

Scene 2

*(*TILMAN *and* RUSS, *and* NAYRON *and* SIENNA *are partners in a game of bid whist.* GINA *and* LA HONDA. LA HONDA *and* SIENNA *are wearing cameos.)*

SIENNA: Can I ask someone a question?

RUSS: Gina, you cut the cards...pretty women bring luck.

NAYRON: Not an ugly woman on this boat.

SIENNA: Does...anyone...know...where...this boat is headed?

RUSS: What kind of question is that? ...Deal.

SIENNA: I told you. I haven't played bid whist in years.

NAYRON: S'alright. Just follow my lead. Just watch what I put down on the table and whatever you do, don't cut me.

TILMAN: You better watch out for her. That's exactly what she will do, man. I'm telling ya straight. She'll cut your cards. I bid three.

NAYRON: How do you know? You two know each other?

SIENNA: Slightly. Years ago. On another cruise.

NAYRON: *(Smiling brightly at* SIENNA*)* Baby, you dealt me a l-o-u-s-y hand. Lousy!

TILMAN: Look at that smile on his face. You not bluffing me. You probably holding fist full of aces.

GINA: Have you noticed that there's no one on the ship but us? No captain, no crew, just us and...

(Enter LEGBA *pretending to swab the deck as he goes from player to player looking over their shoulders at their cards.)*

GINA: ...him.

LEGBA: *(Looking at* NAYRON*'s cards)* I see you planning to dig a few graves with those cards of yours.

NAYRON: Stop signifying my hand, man. Are you crazy? I'm gonna take one of these spades I'm holding and deck you in the head. Stop broadcasting my hand.

LEGBA: *(Goes to each player)* Life is but a game of cards. Some turn a high card at the top while others turn a low. *(To* RUSS*)* When hearts are trumps we play for love. *(To* SIENNA*)* With diamonds you better stake your gold. *(To* TILMAN*)* Clubs look out for war. *(Turns back to* NAYRON*)* You'll find the spade turns up at last and digs every players' grave.

(They all go after LEGBA.*)*

LEGBA: *Pa touche mwen!*

GINA: Russ! It's only a card game... Let him go.

RUSS: If I take the time to play, then I take the time to win.

LA HONDA: I agree. Play to win or not at all. Whatta creep.

TILMAN: *(To* LA HONDA*)* How about kissing me for good luck?

NAYRON: Let that clown go and finish the game. Whose bid was it anyhow?

*(*LEGBA *resumes swabbing the deck.)*

LA HONDA: Russ, can you teach me to play cards? I learn real fast.

TILMAN: *(Doubled over with sudden pain)* It's nothing... nothing...something I ate...goes...and comes. I'll be alright. I'm...gonna...be fine...as...wine...in...no...time...

LA HONDA: Here's a drink of water.

TILMAN: *(Takes the glass from her and drinks it all down.)* I feel better. What was in that water? *(To audience)* I hope it wasn't my mother's remedy.

NAYRON: Study long, you study wrong. Your bid, man. You know, Sienna, I don't care where this boat is going or if we ever get off. I just love being around pretty women.

RUSS: That's just why I decided to make this trip. I. After being out in the world it feels so good to come home and find a beautiful woman who can negotiate all the worlds I have to live in. Four no trump, chumps!

NAYRON: Yessiree. You know, my women have always had to be a cut above average. I always followed may mama's rule. "Son," she said, "son, don't get no woman uglier than you 'cause I want some pretty grandbabies. Even when I was an outlaw I never lost that thought. I always followed mama's rule.

RUSS: Four no trump, chumps!

NAYRON: Four no trumps? No way, Jose! Five no trump. High card wins.

TILMAN: I told ya he was jiving... I knew he was holding a fistful of aces! Shoulda listened to the steward.

NAYRON: *(To* SIENNA*)* I'll lay 'em down, baby, you pick 'em up.

SIENNA: I got your back.

TILMAN: Well, I might lose at cards this trip, but not at love. *(Gazing at* LA HONDA*)* I have found someone to hug up with. Someone with tempo. Someone bright...

SIENNA: *(Laughing to audience)* Bright not as in cleverness, bright not as in mental sharpness, but bright as in damn near—

LA HONDA: Some folks always trying to blame me for looking good.

SIENNA: *(To* TILMAN*)* After all these years, I would think you would be slowing down.

TILMAN: Sweetheart, I'm just like good peppa sauce. I get hotter with age.

NAYRON: Yes, sir. Like I was saying, not a coal shoveler on this entire boat. No need for egg white and lemon juice, hey baby.

LA HONDA: Like I always say, WE LOOK GOOD!

GINA: Were trapped.

LA HONDA: What are you talking about? trapped.

GINA: I feel it...there's something...strange...about this boat.... Like I've been on it...many times...before... making the same trip over and ov—

RUSS: *(Laughing)* Yeah...right... Maybe we're all dead and... and... Yeah... and all us dead black ghostusus are on this...phantom slave ship and, and we' re—I know... I got it. We sailing on the Ethiopic Sea down through the centuries—

NAYRON: With a cargo of tobacco and, and, and cotton...and rum...

TILMAN: *(Fake English accent)* And calicos, and silks...

RUSS: Yeah...to...to barter for, for studs and yellow wenches... No, I got it... How 'bout this... *We* are the studs and *y'all* are the wenches!

(All three men are doubled over with laughter.) Stop it, please... Gina, you are too fine to be so crazy!

NAYRON: You got that right, bro. Gina, girl, You are one P-R-E-T-T-Y fox. Just look at you!

RUSS: You got that right, bro! Gina, you are soooo lucky. Shhheet, I'm thirty-seven-point-four percent Irish, twenty-two percent French, and twelve-and-a-half percent Choctaw. But who would know? I got *all* my dad's features. Good thing I'm a man.

TILMAN: Yeah. We all got something in us. I got a little William the Conquerer, on my Jamaican side.

NAYRON: Play your card, man. I'm proud to say I'm the great-great-great-grandson of a child born in 1807 to a slave who, I'm proud to say, was impregnated by Sir Ery Coote, Jamaica's lieutenant governor and distant relative of the Conquerer, I'm proud to say.

LEGBA: *(Thunderous mumbling under his breath) Zot mem, zot bet, zot mem, zot bet...*

RUSS: What's that you said? What's he mumbling about?

NAYRON: Well, like I always say, be proud of your roots.

LEGBA: It's not your roots that's got you people worried...just your flowers...

RUSS: What that you just said?

LEGBA: I said, don't forget we dine at the captain's table in an hour.

RUSS I mean it. What's that you just said?

LEGBA: I said, don't forget we di—

RUSS: That's not what you said. I heard you. Now look here, man. You're the servant class around here...got that? only a servant. Where's the captain? Take me to him. I want to lodge a formal complaint to the captain about your behavior.

SIENNA: I've been looking for the captain of this ship since I got on board.

LA HONDA: Y'all laugh, but Gina is right. What direction is this boat going?

TILMAN: *(Putting his arms around* LA HONDA*)* Don't worry, You're safe with me. I'm an old sea dog.

SIENNA: *(To audience)* He got the last part right.

TILMAN: I know about winds and currents. I've been in a number of West Indian Sea squalls, a water spout in the China Sea, some submarine encounters during the war...and I think we're going due south-west...

NAYRON: My game! We win.... Y'all didn't make one book. Told y'all I was taken you to Boston. *(To* TILMAN*)* Okay, okay. I know it's only a game. What did you say about the boat, man? What direction did you say we were gain'?

LA HONDA: Hey, Steward. Steward Legba. I demand you tell us right now. In what direction are

we traveling?

LEGBA: *D'espirit,* you all, *d'espirit.*

LA HONDA: Where?

LEGBA: *Vous enbarke kan bateau d'espirit!*

RUSS: What kind of answer is that? Speak English!

LEGBA: Your mind. This boat is travelling only in the direction of your mind.

(End of Scene 2)

Scene 3

(The ship's ballroom. RUSS *in evening clothes. With great ceremony he pins a cameo brooch on* GINA*'s gown. As they dance blood pours from the brooch throughout the scene.)*

GINA: Ouch!

RUSS: When I die...

GINA: I don't know...if I know how to do this...

RUSS: I only want to be handled by you...when I die.

GINA: Faster, stay with the music... move your feet....

RUSS: Like this? Nothing hard against my dead flesh.

GINA: How did you do that? bid you bend the knee and twirl?

RUSS: Only your soft tears to cleanse my sins away.

GINA: Or spin...and then bend?

RUSS: Your lips on my mouth to purify my last breath.

GINA: On, now I get it, side to side and then dip.

RUSS: Your smell in my nostrils. Sprinkle Lavender, lime,and lemon grass on my dead flesh. Call me Dude of Death.

GINA: That little two-step...between stop and go...I—

RUSS: Clean out my cadaver. Plant fruits and flowers in my pelvis.

GINA: When we spin around like this, I get dizzy.

RUSS: Feed me to the stars.

GINA: Your feet. So fast. You're leaving the music. Wait.

RUSS: Can't.

GINA: Hold on, wait. I'm coming.

(End of scene 3)

Scene 4

(The Chocolate Singles are seated at the captain's table dressed in black-tie, waiting for the Captain to appear.)

TILMAN: The captain of this ship has all of our lives in his hands and we don't even know—

GINA: The steward told me—

RUSS: That clown! I don't know why you even let him talk to you.

GINA: I like him. He reminds me of my Uncle Crazy. *(To audience)* Everyone called him "Uncle Crazy" because he used to go around asking everyone,

LEGBA: *(Voice over)* "Why don't you see the same shit as I see" See the same shit as I see and see that is see that I see and what I see is that I see something icy and cold and hard and I don't want to have jack shit to do with that jack shit. Godman goddamn goddman The Man and his cold hand.

(Pause)

GINA: Uncle Crazy...I think I take after him.

NAYRON: Personally, I would like to bust him one. It's a good thing I'm rehabilitated else I would bust him one. He got 'tude galore.

TILMAN: Our invitations said seven.

RUSS: I never wait for anyone this long—

LA HONDA: Russ, I'm thirsty. Can you order us drinks while we wait for His Honor?

GINA: He's a ship captain, not a judge.

LA HONDA: So what? It *is* an honor to be invited to the captain's table.

SIENNA: Wonder why he chose us to dine, just, just us tonight?

LA HONDA: Maybe...'cause there's no one else around. Gina's and Sienna are right. I began to suspect something. Nobody seems to know where we are going. I'd forgotten myself though I didn't want to admit it. So I got out of my cabin and went over the ship. Yes, all over her. Into the officers' quarters and everything. No one said a word to me for a very simple reason. There's no one on board to say anything. No, no captain, no crew, no nothing, just us and...Legba.

GINA: Last night the wind sounded like human moans.

RUSS: You couldn't find a more luxurious ship. Hand-laid mosaics, lustrous woods, art deco murals, European cuisine.

GINA: Yes, it's coated with gold and glitter with the finest appointments except for the stink from the hole.

RUSS: Your imagination is as intense as your fair beauty. This luxury cruiser is state-of-the-art. Fresh flowers everywhere.

GINA: Last night this ship tossed and raced like mad like demons were chasing it.

RUSS: Just your imagination.

GINA: My stomach churned like the sea. I heard chains rattling and folks moaning and babies crying and babies crying and babies crying and then "splasssshhhh" as something hit the water... and then.... nothing.

(A silence from all of them.)

NAYRON: Hey, babee. Cheer up and chill out. This is the 21st Century. Credit cards in our pockets. Pretty women on our arms. We the cruisers now. Not the cargo.

GINA: And the clanking, clanking, clanking of chains seem to come from the ship's hole.

NAYRON: Damn, baby, you really were seasick weren't you?

RUSS: Stop it, Gina. Just stop it now! Next thing you'll be telling us is that you have been stumbling over branding irons and whips. Forget the past. let's just grab the moment' am sick of history. I hate the past! *(He puts his arm around* GINA*)* Don't you understand why I'm on this Singles Cruise?' just want to be a normal person with a pretty woman and our pretty children. No different from any other hard-working man trying to make it.

NAYRON: Say, bro— Now I know. I been looking at you, wondering where I've seen your face—and now I remember. You all over the place, T V, Internet... I've heard all about you—lessee. Yeah, what's the name of your company again...?

RUSS: "Civilization...Inc."

NAYRON: That's right. Yeah, yeah. I've seen your ads. "Welcome to Civilization. Step up, sir. Your drink is waiting."

RUSS: The right image is crucial. Our clients want to let everyone know they have made it..

NAYRON: My main man. So you the H N I C.

RUSS: New alaphabet my brothuh. C E O. I own the company. H N I C is old time boogie.

LA HONDA: I knew it. I bet you go first class all the way. I bet your stateroom is a mansion at sea.

RUSS: OhhhhhhNo. Nothing like that—

NAYRON: Why don't you invite us up to see it, bro. How many berths in it you got, man?

RUSS: Aww. It only sleeps ten.

NAYRON: In your own cabin? Ten berths? Man, that's not a berth. That's a litter!

(They all crack up and LEGBA *enters, now dressed as an elegant waiter in a French restaurant. He is very much taller than previously, his body pumped up, gestures flamboyant, which makes him a mixture of a body builder and Liberace. He waits silently with his order pad.)*

LA HONDA: *(Looking at* RUSS*)* I'll drink...whatever he's drinking.

RUSS: *(Looking at* GINA*)* A bottle of your whitest wine, *blanc et blanc* for the lady and me.

LA HONDA: Me too.

TILMAN: I thought you told me you hated wine.

LEGBA: White wine for the lady. But of course, white wine for everyone. But non, I don't think so.

RUSS: Maybe you didn't hear... *Blanc et blanc* for each and every one of us.

LEGBA: *C'est impossible. Non!* No drinks before dinner! Bad for ze appetite!

ALL: I'm gonna kick yo—
What the hell!

LEGBA: *(Backing away from them) Kol pa! Pa touche mwen!* Don't come near me, don't touch me I see that you are unhappy. I go get El Capitano.

*(*LEGBA *hurriedly exits. The Captain appears in full-dress uniform, his face hidden by a beard and sunglasses. There*

is a fixed grin [or grimace] on this face as he bows stiffly to each diner. He puffs on an exaggeratedly long, thick cigar, silently blows stinking cigar into the diner's face. The audience, but not the diners, are aware that the Captain is LEGBA *in disguise.)*

TILMAN: *(Slapping the Captain on his back.)* So, Capin. What kind of weather are you giving us? HehHeh.

SIENNA: Silly, you think the Captain ladles out weather each day like soup.

(Awkward silence)

GINA: Tell us, sir. What was the *S S Chiaroscuro* before it was refurbished. What is this ship's history?

TILMAN: Captain...Captain. Can you explain the ship's course to us. Of course, being an old sailor myself, I told them—but we need an expert's advice.

(Another awkward silence)

TILMAN: Ah, yes, never mind, Cap' n. Never mind their bad temper. They are all a little seasick. It's been a rough tri— But, Captain...we'd like to introduce ourselves...even though we don't know *your* name.

RUSS: I don't give a damn what your name is. You can never be found. Nobody knows your name. After what seems like centuries, you finally invite us to your table, but there's no food. You show up hours late and pollute the air with your stinking cigar. Are we passengers or sl—or what, man? And about your steward—that Legba dude? He doesn't know his place. What is his place? Where are we going and when will we get there? Are standing still? Are we moving. It's hard to tell. It seems that on your ship, motion doesn't mean advancement. We are going nowhere fast and gaining no ground. Two steps forward, ten steps backwards. You call this progress?

(The "captain" maintains his silence and his grin as he looks from one to another, puffing away. He suddenly gets up, bows stiffly and exits.)

GINA: I don't think the Captain speaks English.

RUSS: At least not to us.

(Enter LEGBA *as the uppity waiter. He walks past the diners to center and faces the audience. All his lines are delivered to the back row as if he is auditioning.)*

LEGBA: *(In a deep, booming voice)* EL CAPITANO CAPTAIN-SENDS-SENDS-HIS-APOLOGIES. PLEASE TO EXCUSE. THE THE-CAPTAIN IS EXPECTORATING.

LA HONDA: *(Leaning over to* TILMAN *and whispering)* Gee, I thought that only happened to women!

LEGBA: *(Still facing audience)* YOUR-ORDERS-PLEASE.

SIENNA: We don't have menus.

LA HONDA: I am thoroughly sick of him!

LEGBA: *(Still facing the audience)* ONE, FOR YOUR SICKNESS WE HAVE THE SEA. TWO, AS FOR YOUR DRINKS—*NON*. THREE, YOU DON'T-NEED-MENUS. I-WILL-TELL-YOU-WHAT-IS-ON-LA-MENU. BUT-FIRST-BEFORE-YOU-ORDER-I-MU ST-COLLECT-YOUR-MONEE.

ALL: Man, you need to be jacked up, bad!
Get out of town!
Shit!
Motherfucker!

LEGBA: *(Feigning surprise) MON-DIEU!* BUT-DO-YOU-THINK-YOU-CAN-SIT-AT-THE-CAPTAIN'S-TABLE-FREE?

RUSS: No one pays to sit at the captain's table. We were invited.

LEGBA: *(Turns around and looks at the diners for the first time.)* YOU were invited? Hmmmmmmmmf! *(Faces the audience once more) La speciale* for the *diner* with discriminating taste there is a lovely white fleshed fish, seasoned with white vinegar, white peppercorns, white salt, white onions, and served with white potatoes, topped off with white bread. *(He remains smirking at the audience as the diners order.)*

RUSS: What else is there?

LEGBA: *Rien.*

NAYRON: Get us whatever you have, dude. We're starving. And I'm warning you—you better check yo'self before you wreck yo'self.

RUSS: Wait till I see my travel agent.

LEGBA: *(Bowing deeply)* One other thing...El Capitano has invited you to his play.

NAYRON: Yeah, yeah...just bring us our orders. We are all very hungry.

LEGBA: El Capitano has arranged that you enjoy every moment of your journey.

TILMAN: The food, man. The food. Bring us the food.

LEGBA: May I tell him you all agree?

ALL: Yeah. Sure. Fine. Okay. Anything.

Hungry. We'll go to the damned play. We'll go!

LEGBA: I'm afraid you don't understand.You're expected...to...participate...to act in it. On this ship...it's always done...

RUSS: Anything, boss, anything. Sure we'll be glad to sing, tap dance, juggle, act. FEED US.

LEGBA: Then...I can tell him...to...ex—

(NAYRON moves toward him threateningly and LEGBA *makes a fast exit.)*

TILMAN: I was an actor... Once...a long time ago.

NAYRON: I always wanted to be one.

GINA: Sounds like fun. I wonder what play?

TILMAN: Now I remember...I saw a poster—it said... said...I think it said...

LA HONDA: I know...I know...don't tell me...I know... it's that black play, Othello.

(At this moment LEGBA *enters, very friendly and very humble and solicitious to the waiting diners.)*

LEGBA: My deepest apologies. The Captain has reassured me you are his invited and honored guests. *(He sits down in the Captain's seat.)* The Captain sends his regret at his delay. He asked me to *informe* you that he is, indeed, micturating.

TILMAN: Ah yes. I remember that from my old sea days. A big ship like this needs micturating constantly.

RUSS: Hey, bro. Let me pull your coat. That means the Captain is taking a leak.

NAYRON: Why are you sitting down at our table?

LEGBA: A cat may sit with a king, *mais non*? A mosquito may sit on an elephant, *non*? A waiter may sit with the diners. N'est pas?

NAYRON: *(Grabbing* LEGBA*)* You tell your micturating Captain I am going to defecate on you if you don't get the hell out of here and bring us our food.

*(*LEGBA *escapes, hurries out and comes right back, bringing in steaming covered trays. He sets the trays before them. Reseats the diners. Orders everyone around so that finally all the men are seated together.)*

LEGBA: You must sit over there, *la*...and you, next to him, *la la*. Over here, *mademoiselle*, next to her. And you over here. *Bon*.

(They all meekly obey and after they are re-seated LEGBA *looks them satisfied.)*

LEGBA: *(Travels from diner to diner laying a covered dish before each of them) Bon, c'est si bon.* You had the lovely white fleshed fish seasoned with white vinegar, white peppercorns, white salt, whole white potatoes, served with white bread.

ALL: *(Impatient with hunger)* That's right. Correct. Yes, yes, get on with it, man.

LEGBA: *Non. N'est pas.* There is none. *C'est impossible.* There is none of what you orderrrrrrred.

ALL: But you told us it was on the menu.

LEGBA: I lied. All waiters are liar. However. Don't despair. El Capitano say for me to wish you *bon voyage* and *bon appetit.*

ALL: *(Lifting the covers from the trays)* Where's our food? What is this crap? Are you crazy? I didn't order this!

LEGBA: Egg white and lemon juice for the ladies. Whip cream and vanilla ice cream for the men. EAT UP!

(A melee ensues where all try to attack LEGBA. *Instead the vanilla ice cream spills on everyone. As they all try to wipe it off themselves,* LEGBA *pretends to help them, but he is really spreading the white cream all over everyone's faces until they all end up in white face.)*

(Tableau as they gaze white-faced at the audience.)

LEGBA: *(Bowing to the audience)* El Capitano says, "Accidents reveal the man."

(End of Scene 3)

Scene 4

(LEGBA cartwheels on stage. Dressed as a jester in a clown costume, one side of him black, the other white. He has a red nose painted on his face.

LEGBA: *(To audience)* Blackamoors, fair maidens... and others. Welcome to our play, *Crazy for You,* a modern adaptation of that famous love story of the Moor and his fair Desdemona. And while we weep for Desdemona, what about Shaneekwa? Poor girl. *Tout la mizer ye to fe li*—all the hardships she doth endure.
"I'm crazy for you, Desdemona,"
Cry all the Moors
While Shaneekwa, from shore to shore,
Bewails her lot with bitter sighs,
Unbeloved dark daughter of burning skies.

She sends her cries unto the skies:
"I am cursed. O heaven above
My hue seems not the color of love.

Scorned for fairer creatures born,
Shaneekwa endures all kinds of scorn.
Whether high or low, near or far,
Not one seems to like the dark.
There is one belief all seem to share:
No woman is Ugly that is Fair.
And this they whisper...or...loudly state:
A Fair woman is just too pretty to hate.
May the gods help actors the truth to reveal
Words not meant to separate, but to heal.
(Looking around for GINA*)*
Now we all know the story of the Moor's love for his fair Desdemona.

*(*GINA *enters.)*

GINA: I told you I don't want to play this part. I have got to talk to you, Russ.

LEGBA: *(To* GINA*)* Assume the character, please. Our comedy has begun.

GINA: No. I don't want to play Desdemona! Russ, help me.

RUSS: One of us playing the fair Venetian princess. This is a first. You should be proud, girl.

GINA: Well, I'm not. I'm not trying to be a snob, but the truth is I'm longing to play a real black woman

RUSS: Face it, pretty woman. You don't exactly look like Aunt Jemima.

*(*GINA *recoils as if struck.)*

(Enter LA HONDA *and* SIENNA *dressed as ladies-in-waiting.)*

LADIES-IN-WAITING:
Pale Desdemona,
Your liquid locks falling and flipping and flying,
It is Venus' error
That you are nearer Earth than is wont
And drive Moors mad.

GINA: Stop this. Stop!

LADIES-IN-WAITING:
And we are but sooty shadows.

GINA: I am what I am not! I can't play Desdemona. I'm telling you, I don't look like her.

LADIES-IN-WAITING:
Pretty Desdemona
The Moors far and wide
Are crazy for you
For when love is on the mind
All the women are fair
While all the men are dark
And some of us don't feel so brave.

GINA: NO. STOP IT. I don't want this part. I will not play that silly bitch besdemona. And I never liked Othello.

RUSS/OTHELLO:
(Throws away his script as he goes. toward GINA*)*
Why fair maiden mine
Why, why fairest of the fair,
When I do love thee so?
Your pretty visage is ever before me.
I fear nothing, save the loss
Of my fair love.
The pearl-like luster of your pretty skin:
It's pale glow adorns my day,
Lights up dark night.

Yet unstained and unblemished,
Unconquered by the darkness,
Your beauty is abloom.
Your beauty, fair goddess, is
A virtue, no an elixir, no a calmative, no a balm,
Nay, not one, 'tis all of these.
The pretty light from your eyes
Dazzles, blinds my dark orbs.
For you are all things bright and good and beautiful
And fair.

GINA/DESDEMONA:
Answer me this, beloved Othello,
I wonder, noble Moor,
If you would love me
If I were black like you?

RUSS/OTHELLO:
But you are not
In sooth
You query must needs me remained moot!

GINA/DESDEMONA:
Does it follow that we must abhor

Those with whom we share like hue?
If you were white, my blackamoor,
Methinks I'd love you still.
Even if, alas, you were not
Your glorious dark,
Even if your wooly, curly, kinky kinks,
Limp and straight
Even if your ebon lips were pale and thin
Instead of dark and thick and full and wide....
I'd love you still.

RUSS/OTHELLO:
That so fair a pretty maiden
Can love me
And see me lovely in her eye
All the taunts of those that called me ugly Fade
Because in me you see love
God bless these modern times when I can boldly say
Without fear of rope or bullet,
I love you...
Nobody but you my pretty maiden
Because, well you know,
A black face like mine
Often shelters a heart as white as snow!

GINA/DESDEMONA: Listen, Russ...I mean...Othello... dammit, I mean both of you. I'm trying to tell you, I may be fair, but I am dark.
I am white, but black.
Black and comely

RUSS/OTHELLO: But your image before me gives me content And satisfies my eye's appetite with fullness.

LADIES-IN-WAITING:
When love is on the mind
All the women are fair,
All the men are dark—
But sometimes some of us don't feel so brave....

*(*TILMAN *and* NAYRON *enter as* MEN OF ARMS.*)*

MEN-OF-ARMS:
Stuff and nonsense, colorist trash!
Poppycock and balderdash!
Ye women of sable hue,
Look here, I'll give it to you straight.
An ugly woman is an ugly woman
And a fair woman just too pretty to hate!

NAYRON: I like what I like...no apologies. I'm a free man.

GINA/DESDEMONA:
O Blackamoors, it seems to me
You freed men now have the vaules of slavery.

LADIES-IN-WAITING:
It's plain to see in reality...
It's plain to see that in reality-
It's plain to see that in reality—what...is happening?

(All are horrified as they look at GINA *who is slowly turning into her natural darker self.)*

GINA/DESDEMONA:
(Slowly walks toward RUSS *as she is reverting)*
Because hate is legislated,
(She pauses. Every time she pauses her skin and hair return to their natural state bit by bit.)
And only love can turn the tide,
(Pause)
I need love more than ever now.
(To audience)
I need your love.

RUSS: What's wrong with you?
What's going on?

ALL: Get a doctor, she must be dying.
Are you in pain? Does it hurt?

Gangrene is setting in.
Her hair. Those lips. She musta been poisoned.

(GINA attempts to escape.)

RUSS: What point are you trying to prove?

LA HONDA: What a neat trick.

(RUSS staring at GINA)

LA HONDA:
You may remove the tincture from your face,
The thick from your lips,
The kink from your hair...

GINA: It doesn't come off.

LEGBA: *(To audience)*
Is brown Desdemona fair?
Now that her face is pure ebony
I ask...does beauty in her seem to lack?

RUSS: Shut the fuck up! You know about this, didn't you? You knew all the time that she was passing... didn't you?

LEGBA: I am only a lowly steward on the slave ship of your mind.

GINA: Like or dislike me?
Choose you
Never mind the outward skin
That holds the jewels deep within.

RUSS: Talk normal, dammit. Speak plainly. To hell with Desdemona and Othello. This shit is real!

(GINA silence.)

RUSS: You better talk to me, girl. I want some answers. How could you do such a thing. Talk, I said.

GINA: This is really me. This is what I really look like.

RUSS: I don't give a damn what shade your sk— Hey! How could you try a cheap trick like this? What kind of man do you think I am?

GINA: A successful man, who loves life. A tender man who loves being around women. A strong man who made me feel treasured. The man I came on this cruise to meet. A man I want.

RUSS: What kind of superficial person do you think I am?

GINA: It's not that, honest, Russ. When I decided to go on this Chocolate Singles Cruise I was determined to find somebody.

RUSS: I loved you, Gina. I loved you.

GINA: And now...you don't?

RUSS: Don't be silly. Of course I do. You think just because you're... But you *did* deceive me. Put yourself in my place.

GINA: I can't. You are a man. I looked around and who was being asked out for dates, who was getting married, and my eyes and common sense told me to prepare for a single life. But...I just couldn't.

RUSS: So you decided to use deception. When were you going to tell me? So you decided to use deception. When were you going to tell me?

GINA: Way before this treatment wore off. At least that's what I had planned. I am definitely getting my money back. Every last penny.

RUSS: It's not your color that I'm angry about...it's the deception...believe me. I've always prided myself in being colorblind. I just don't see color.... To me, it makes no difference and everybody's the same. Really. But I can't understand how you could—just tell me why.

GINA: Okay...okay... Lemme...I'll try and explain...I come from a family of daughters. Six unmarried sisters and their children. We have big dining roomtable. We stopped cooking a long time ago, what with school and work. We just order take-out together and sit down with linen napkins and chinaware, just like we cooked the store-bought meal from scratch. Afterwards we all pile up in one big bed, me and my sisters and their children all tangled up in one another so we don't even know whose arms and legs belong to what body. And all the time I am laughing with them, I'm thinking, "Where are the men? What happened to the men in this family?"

RUSS: Honest, baby. I am really trying to understand, but I swear I don't. What are you trying to tell me. I don't get it. How could you pass yourself off as...you know...when you are really...you are really...you know what *I* mean.

GINA: I'm trying to tell you. I'ts...hard to talk about 'cause no one does, but it was easy once I...really... read...the...signs.

RUSS: What do you mean the signs? What signs?

GINA: The signs...they're all around...in the air. All around. Internet. Billboards. M T V. The brothers, the sisters, the sisters, the movies, my family...it's in the air...all around. It follows me out of the house...into the streets...slips into the letters of every alphabet that I hear. It's in everyone's eyes. It seems, seems... sorta...I think...I thought...kinda...I believe...my belief is... it's all around...everyone is colorblind...so they say... maybe I was self cons— ...You know what I mean. You know like... I mean...like all the men in my family...you know...they all marry...know what I mean? It doesn not matter they—you know...it does not matter they say all the time...but I see it does matter to them. A lot.

"What difference does it make?" they all say. "It make no difference" ...Yet the color of one's skin is a part of ourselves. It is precious and yet it should not matter and it does matter even though everyone says that it doesn't...I feel like—that's how I felt. I just feel—I might be wrong. I know...that I'm not. I wish that I was...but I'm no—

RUSS: I still don't see how you coul—

GINA: Because I need love and why shouldn't I? Because I'm lonely, lonely. I'm lonely and I want someone like you to talk to. Okay? That's why I did it... and it worked...for awhile. D'you think we can talk... now. Could we continue? Now...do you understand?

(End of Scene 4)

Scene 5

(The gangplank is down. The Chocolate Singles are debarking from the ship. LEGBA, *dressed in his steward's uniform, bids them farewell as they descend.)*

TILMAN: Ahoy I smell land..

LEGBA: Alright, sailor. It's time debark. Time to climb off the ark.

TILMAN: Riddle me this, Leba. Why is every woman in the world except one woman always sad after making love? *(Pauses)* That's easy. 'Cause I'm only one man and there's not enough of me to go around! Ahhhhhhshiit.

*(*LEGBA *laughs but doubles over and is caught in the grip of pain.)*

TILMAN: *(Handling* LEGBA *a piece of paper)* DAMN! Give this to Sienna for me, please. I have to hurry. I have a very important appointment that can't put off any longer. *Au revoir.*

*(*TILMAN *descends down the gangplank as* GINA *appears.)*

LEGBA: How lovely you look this morning, miss. Just as I always pictured you.

GINA: Just tell me one thing... How did you know?

LEGBA: I been sailing up and down these seas for centuries.

GINA: Soon it will only be a dream—or nightmare, or a memory and all I will wonder is...why?

*(*RUSS *rushes up to* GINA*)*

RUSS: I've been looking all over...for you. Where were you.

GINA: Here I am.

RUSS: *(Pause)* I just wanted to say...goo— I will always remember leaning on the rail with my arms around you and the lights from the shore getting smaller and smaller while the music played and we danced and—and...and...

GINA: Me too...

RUSS: I just wanted to say...

GINA: Me too...

RUSS: I like you the way you are—

GINA: You don't have—

RUSS: No, really. I mean, Gina. Really...I like...you... It doesn't ma—

GINA: —to say that...it's not a dis—

RUSS: No. I mean really.

GINA: *(Extends her hand for a friendly handshake)* Nice meeting you.

RUSS: Truth is...I'm glad we're back on land. I never did like being on a boat much. Being hemmed in. The sky and the sea blurred together without outlines, without a bottom, without a top and no horizon, just endless fog and shifting mist. Not knowing left, right, up or down. All that water. Glad to be back on land. *(Pause)* Lemme give you my number...call me sometime.

GINA: Right!

*(*RUSS *kisses* GINA *on the cheek and runs down the gangplank, but turns once more to wave at her and disappears.)*

LEGBA: My dear, now he was never the man for you. You need a man who can appreciate your beauty. A man like me.

GINA: I've heard about you sea-faring men.

LEGBA: It's just a male thang. A woman wouldn't understand.

LA HONDA: Gina, here's my card. Let's talk. I'll be straight with you. Before I used to think you thought you was cute. But now...well now, we can be friends. *(Suddenly gives* GINA *a kiss and hands her a card)* Give me a call...Sister.

LEGBA: Au revoir, Miss La Honda. Did I ever tell you how beautiful you are?

LA HONDA: *(Genuinely touched)* I didn't think you noticed. I didn't think you even liked me.

LEGBA: How could I keep my eyes off those beautiful, luscious, full, shiny, wet lips of yours.

LA HONDA: Thank you.

LEGBA: Did you know that lips on the mouth of a female are a reflection of lips on another part of the female anatomy? Know what I mean?

LA HONDA *(Grabbing* LEGBA*'s hands)* I don't suppose you want to tell me wht these short, stubby fingers of yours are a reflection of? Know what I mean? Bye bye!

GINA: *(Laughing)* She gotcha!

(Enter NAYRON *and* SIENNA *arm in arm.)*

NAYRON: Hey, bro. This trip was mind-expanding. I feel like I set foot on some mystic harbor or something... And that play...was the bomb. That Shakespeare...

SIENNA: I keep telling you...that was an adaptation... not the real—

NAYRON: ..was deep. I think I want to act. I betcha I could play Othello.

LEGBA: I think so too.

SIENNA: —Oh well, let's just take the ferry next time.

NAYRON: Next time? No more single cruises for you, mama.

SIENNA: I am not your mother.

NAYRON: You got that right, mama.

LEGBA Tilman gave me this note to give to you.

*(*SIENNA *takes it and reads it.)*

NAYRON: What's it say?

SIENNA: *(Reading the note)* Nothing. Everything.

NAYRON: Let me see. *(Reading the note)* "Will you marry me? Will you marry me?" Say, what's going on? Talk to me, Mama,

SIENNA: It's just a silly game... Let's go...Daddy.

GINA: *(To audience)* Don't worry. Bye bye. I'm going home, refigure this thing called "love" and take a long, long look in my mirr—

LEGBA: *(Bowing to audience)*
Our mirror is the root of all comedy
It never lies; It never tells the truth.
The Mirror is merely reflective

While our shadow tells us we're only
A matter of perspective.
Can't you see? Don't you agree,
Our image is not a stone cold fact?
For flesh can lighten, darken, expand, contract
And I proclaim without control
There is no true beauty but the soul!
(Pause)
I remain your humble servant, Paul Paul Legba, otherwise known as Papa or *(Bows low and takes off her disguise and reveals herself as a woman)* Mama Legbal.

(Curtain)

END OF PLAY

www.ingramcontent.com/pod-product-compliance
Lightning Source LLC
LaVergne TN
LVHW020659100826
845148LV00012B/2563

* 9 7 8 0 8 8 1 4 5 4 7 2 7 *